People in My Community/La gente de mi comunidad

Police Officer/
El policía

Jacqueline Laks Gorman
photographs by/fotografías de Gregg Andersen

Reading consultant/Consultora de lectura: Susan Nations, M.Ed., author/literacy coach/consultant

WEEKLY WR READER®
EARLY LEARNING LIBRARY

Please visit our web site at: **www.earlyliteracy.cc**
For a free color catalog describing Weekly Reader® Early Learning Library's
list of high-quality books, call 1-877-445-5824 (USA) or 1-800-387-3178 (Canada).
Weekly Reader® Early Learning Library's fax: (414) 336-0164.

Library of Congress Cataloging-in-Publication Data

Gorman, Jacqueline Laks, 1955-
    [Police officer. Spanish & English]
    Police officer = El policía / by Jacqueline Laks Gorman.
      p. cm. — (People in my community = La gente de mi comunidad)
    Summary: A simple description of what a police officer does, helping people,
stopping people who break the law, and directing traffic.
    Includes bibliographical references and index.
    ISBN 0-8368-3311-2 (lib. bdg.)
    ISBN 0-8368-3345-7 (softcover)
    1. Police—Juvenile literature. 2. Bilingual books. [1. Police. 2. Occupations.
3. Spanish language materials—Bilingual.] I. Title: Policía. II. Title.
HV7922.G6718   2002
363.2—dc21
                                      2002066367

This edition first published in 2002 by
Weekly Reader® Early Learning Library
330 West Olive Street, Suite 100
Milwaukee, WI 53212 USA

Art direction and page layout: Tammy Gruenewald
Photographer: Gregg Andersen
Editorial assistant: Diane Laska-Swanke
Production: Susan Ashley
Translators: Tatiana Acosta and Guillermo Gutiérrez

Printed in the United States of America

1 2 3 4 5 6 7 8 9 08 07 06 05 04

Note to Educators and Parents

Reading is such an exciting adventure for young children! They are beginning to integrate their oral language skills with written language. To encourage children along the path to early literacy, books must be colorful, engaging, and interesting; they should invite the young reader to explore both the print and the pictures.

People in My Community is a new series designed to help children read about the world around them. In each book young readers will learn interesting facts about some familiar community helpers.

Each book is specially designed to support the young reader in the reading process. The familiar topics are appealing to young children and invite them to read — and re-read — again and again. The full-color photographs and enhanced text further support the student during the reading process.

In addition to serving as wonderful picture books in schools, libraries, homes, and other places where children learn to love reading, these books are specifically intended to be read within an instructional guided reading group. This small group setting allows beginning readers to work with a fluent adult model as they make meaning from the text. After children develop fluency with the text and content, the book can be read independently. Children and adults alike will find these books supportive, engaging, and fun!

Una nota a los educadores y a los padres

¡La lectura es una emocionante aventura para los niños! En esta etapa están comenzando a integrar su manejo del lenguaje oral con el lenguaje escrito. Para fomentar la lectura desde una temprana edad, los libros deben ser vistosos, atractivos e interesantes; deben invitar al joven lector a explorar tanto el texto como las ilustraciones.

La gente de mi comunidad es una nueva serie pensada para ayudar a los niños a conocer el mundo que los rodea. En cada libro, los jóvenes lectores conocerán datos interesantes sobre el trabajo de distintas personas de la comunidad.

Cada libro ha sido especialmente diseñado para facilitar el proceso de lectura. La familiaridad con los temas tratados atrae la atención de los niños y los invita a leer — y releer — una y otra vez. Las fotografías a todo color y el tipo de letra facilitan aún más al estudiante el proceso de lectura.

Además de servir como fantásticos libros ilustrados en la escuela, la biblioteca, el hogar y otros lugares donde los niños aprenden a amar la lectura, estos libros han sido concebidos específicamente para ser leídos en grupos de instrucción guiada. Este contexto de grupos pequeños permite que los niños que se inician en la lectura trabajen con un adulto cuya fluidez les sirve de modelo para comprender el texto. Una vez que se han familiarizado con el texto y el contenido, los niños pueden leer los libros por su cuenta. ¡Tanto niños como adultos encontrarán que estos libros son útiles, entretenidos y divertidos!

— Susan Nations, M.Ed., author, literacy coach,
and consultant in literacy development

The police officer
has an important job.
The police officer
helps people.

— — — — — — —

El trabajo del policía
es muy importante.
El policía ayuda a
la gente.

The police officer helps people in trouble. The police officer helps people in danger.

- - - - - - - -

El policía ayuda a la gente en apuros. El policía ayuda a la gente en peligro.

Police officers wear badges and special clothes. They use **radios** to talk to each other.

- - - - - - -

Los policías llevan ropa y distintivos especiales. Usan **radios** para comunicarse.

radio/radio

Police officers stop people who break the law. Sometimes they use **handcuffs**.

— — — — — — — —

Los policías detienen a la gente que no respeta la ley. A veces usan las **esposas**.

handcuffs/esposas

11

Sometimes police officers ride in police cars or on **motorcycles**. Sometimes they ride on horseback.

- - - - - - - -

Algunas veces los policías van en autos o en **motocicletas**. Otras veces van a caballo.

**motorcycles/
motocicletas**

Sometimes police officers direct traffic. They give tickets to drivers who drive too fast.

- - - - - - -

A veces, los policías dirigen el tráfico. Ponen multas a los conductores que manejan muy deprisa.

Sometimes police officers visit schools. They talk to you about keeping safe.

- - - - - - -

A veces, los policías visitan las escuelas. Te explican qué debes hacer para mantenerte seguro.

If you are ever lost or need help, you should talk to a police officer.

Si algunas vez te pierdes o necesitas ayuda, debes hablar con un policía.

It looks like fun to be a police officer. Would you like to be a police officer some day?

- - - - - - -

Ser policía parece divertido. ¿Te gustaría ser policía algún día?

Glossary/Glosario

badges — small signs that identify people and that are pinned to their clothes

distintivos — pequeñas insignias prendidas en la ropa que sirven para identificar a las personas

danger — something that is not safe

peligro — algo que no es seguro

handcuffs — metal rings that are locked around someone's wrists

esposas — anillas de metal que se cierran alrededor de las muñecas de una persona

law — a rule that people follow for the good of everyone

ley — norma que la gente debe respetar para el bien común

For More Information/Más información

Fiction Books/Libros de ficción

Rathmann, Peggy. *Officer Buckle and Gloria.* New York: Putnam, 1995.

Yee, Wong Herbert. *The Officer's Ball.* Boston: Houghton Mifflin, 1997.

Nonfiction Books/Libros de no ficción

Greene, Carol. *Police Officers Protect People.* Plymouth, Minn.: Child's World, 1997.

Kottke, Jan. *A Day with Police Officers.* New York: Children's Press, 2000.

Schaefer, Lola M. *We Need Police Officers.* Mankato, Minn.: Pebble Books, 2000.

Web Sites/Páginas Web

Police Are My Friends Coloring Book
www.hendersonville-pd.org/kids/coloringbook/
A picture book about police officers to print out, read, and color

Index/Índice

About the Author/Información sobre la autora

Jacqueline Laks Gorman is a writer and editor. She grew up in New York City and began her career working on encyclopedias and other reference books. Since then, she has worked on many different kinds of books. She lives with her husband and children, Colin and Caitlin, in DeKalb, Illinois.

Jacqueline Laks Gorman es escritora y editora. Creció en Nueva York, y se inició en su profesión editando enciclopedias y otros libros de consulta. Desde entonces ha trabajado en muchos tipos de libros. Vive con su esposo y sus hijos, Colin y Caitlin, en DeKalb, Illinois.